TAPAS

TAPAS

**Delicious little plates
to share from Spain**

RYLAND PETERS & SMALL
LONDON • NEW YORK

Senior Designer Emily Breen
Senior Editor Abi Waters
Head of Production Patricia Harrington
Creative Director Leslie Harrington
Editorial Director Julia Charles

Indexer Vanessa Bird

First published in 2024
by Ryland Peters & Small
20–21 Jockey's Fields
London WC1R 4BW
and
341 E 116th St
New York NY 10029

www.rylandpeters.com

10 9 8 7 6 5 4 3 2 1

Text copyright © Valerie Aikman-Smith,
Julz Beresford, Ross Dobson, Clare Ferguson,
Jenny Linford, Louise Pickford, Annie Rigg,
Shelagh Ryan, Jennie Shapter, Linda Tubby
and Ryland Peters & Small 2024
Design and photography copyright © Ryland
Peters & Small 2024
(See page 128 for full credits)

ISBN: 978-1-78879-608-8

Printed in China

A CIP record for this book is available from
the British Library.
US Library of Congress Cataloging-in-Publication
Data has been applied for.

NOTES
• Both British (Metric) and American (Imperial plus
US cups) ingredients measurements are included
in these recipes for your convenience, however it
is important to work with one set of measurements
and not alternate between the two within a recipe.
• All spoon measurements are level unless
otherwise specified.
• All eggs are medium (UK) or large (US), unless
specified as large, in which case US extra-large
should be used. Uncooked or partially cooked eggs
should not be served to the very old, frail, young
children, pregnant women or those with
compromised immune systems.
• Ovens should be preheated to the specified
temperatures. We recommend using an oven
thermometer. If using a fan-assisted oven, adjust
temperatures according to the manufacturer's
instructions.
• When a recipe calls for the grated zest of citrus
fruit, buy unwaxed fruit and wash well before
using. If you can only find treated fruit, scrub
well in warm soapy water before using.

Contents

INTRODUCTION

The word 'tapas' stems from the Spanish verb *tapar*, meaning 'to cover'. Legend has it that the tapas tradition began when King Alfonso X of Castile recovered from an illness by drinking wine alongside small dishes in-between meals. He then made it illegal for taverns to serve wine to customers unless it was accompanied by a small snack or *tapa*. The word became a kind of loophole in the law to allow drinkers to consume alcohol.

Tapas have evolved in Spain by incorporating ingredients and influences from several different countries. The invasion of the North African Moors in the 8th century brought almonds, citrus fruits and fragrant spices. The influence of their presence remains today, especially in Andalusia. The discovery of the New World brought tomatoes, sweet (bell) and chilli/chile peppers, corn, beans and potatoes. These crops were all easy to grow thanks to Spain's temperate climate.

Tapas now enjoy worldwide appeal as they are a highly sociable way to eat, making them the perfect choice for sharing. The mouth-watering recipes included in this book are designed to be combined and many can be made ahead. Mix and match the dishes as you please to create a meat-, seafood- or vegetable-orientated menu. Servings are given as part of a tapas spread.

Chapter 1

CHEESE & EGGS

Spanish Potato Tortilla

This quintessentially Spanish dish is made from a few simple ingredients – eggs, potatoes, onions and olive oil – cooked well.

250 ml/1 cup olive oil

300 g/10½ oz. waxy potatoes, peeled, quartered and thinly sliced

1 onion, halved and thinly sliced

6 large (US extra large) eggs

salt and freshly ground black pepper

a 16-cm/6½-inch heavy non-stick frying pan/skillet (measure the base, not the top)

Serves 4

Pour the olive oil into the frying pan/skillet, add the sliced potatoes and onion, cover the pan and cook gently over a low heat until softened but not coloured, stirring now and then. In effect, you're stewing the vegetables in the oil.

While the potatoes are cooking, beat together the eggs in a large bowl and season with salt and freshly ground black pepper.

Strain the potato mixture into a colander, reserving the olive oil for future use. Season the potato mixture lightly with salt and pour the hot vegetables into the beaten eggs, gently mixing together.

Heat 1 tablespoon of the reserved oil in the same frying pan. Add the egg mixture and fry gently for 10–15 minutes until it has set and there is just a small pool of liquid egg on the surface.

Put a plate on top of the pan, turn it upside down, then slide the tortilla onto the plate. Gently slide the tortilla back into the pan and cook for 2 minutes to set the other side. Remove from the pan and serve warm or at room temperature.

Chorizo Tortilla Bites

A tortilla is a baked omelette that can be served hot or cold. Here it is cut into bite-sized squares, which can be picked up with a toothpick.

4 x 60-g/2-oz. fresh chorizo sausages

16 medium (US large) eggs

300 ml/1¼ cups crème fraîche or sour cream

1 tbsp olive oil

1 red onion, finely chopped

1 garlic clove, crushed

130 g/scant 1 cup fresh or frozen peas

1 red (bell) pepper, deseeded and cut into strips

60 g/1¼ cups baby spinach

salt and freshly ground black pepper

Serves 8

Preheat the oven to 180°C (350°F) Gas 4.

Place the sausages on a baking sheet and cook in the oven for 12 minutes. Drain on paper towels and cut into 1-cm/½-inch slices. Cover and set aside.

Reduce the oven temperature to 110°C (225°F) Gas ¼.

Put the eggs in a large bowl with the crème fraîche and lightly whisk to combine. Season and set aside.

Heat the oil in a large non-stick, ovenproof frying pan/skillet set over a low–medium heat. Add the onion and garlic and sauté until soft but not coloured. Add the chorizo, peas and pepper and cook for 2–3 minutes, stirring. Add the spinach and stir until it begins to wilt.

Arrange the mix evenly over the base of the pan and add the egg mixture. Reduce the heat and gently cook the tortilla, using a spatula to run around the outside of the pan. You don't want any colour on the base of the tortilla so keep the temperature low. After about 10 minutes, once it has just set on the bottom and the sides, place the pan in the oven for 15–20 minutes, until lightly golden and just set in the middle. Remove from the oven and set aside to cool for 10 minutes.

Cover the pan with a board and turn it over to release the tortilla. Cut into 4-cm/1½-inch squares and serve.

Baked Eggs Flamenco Style

4 tbsp olive oil

1 onion, finely chopped

1 garlic clove, crushed

125 g/4 oz. cubed panceta

8 tomatoes, skinned, deseeded and chopped

½ tsp oak-smoked sweet Spanish paprika

1 tbsp dry sherry

2 large roasted red (bell) peppers from a jar, cut into small cubes

12 asparagus tips, cooked

50 g/⅓ cup peas, blanched

4 medium (US large) eggs

8 very thin slices of large cured chorizo (about 35 g/ 1½ oz.)

salt and freshly ground black pepper

a large cazuela (terracotta dish), about 20 cm/8 inches diameter, or 4 small ones (optional)

Serves 4

This substantial tapas dish earned its name from the riot of colours on the plate.

Heat the oil in a frying pan/skillet with an ovenproof handle. Add the onion and garlic and sauté over a medium heat for about 7 minutes until soft and just starting to turn golden. Add the panceta and sauté for 3 minutes. Add the tomatoes, paprika and sherry and cook for about 7 minutes until slightly thickened. Season with a little salt and pepper.

Preheat the oven to 200°C (400°F) Gas 6.

Fold the peppers, asparagus and peas into the mixture. If finishing in a cazuela, transfer the vegetables to the dish at this point. Make 4 indentations in the mixture and break in the eggs; swirl the white part slightly and leave the yolks whole. Bake in the preheated oven for about 10 minutes until the eggs have just set.

Meanwhile, heat a second small frying pan and dry-sauté the chorizo on both sides until the oil runs out and the edges are slightly browned.

Arrange the chorizo on top of the dish and serve.

Mushroom & Pepper Tortilla

3 tbsp olive oil

2 potatoes (about 250 g/9 oz.), peeled and thinly sliced

1 small onion, halved and thinly sliced

75 g/3 oz. button mushrooms, sliced

1 orange (bell) pepper, deseeded and cut into strips

5 large (US extra large) eggs

2 tsp chopped fresh oregano

salt and freshly ground black pepper

a 20-cm/8-inch shallow non-stick cake pan

Serves 4

Any tortilla can be served as tapas, but this recipe makes it even easier because it's cooked in the oven. If you want to make it in advance, serve it cold or reheat for a few minutes in a medium oven.

Preheat the oven to 200°C (400°F) Gas 6.

Pour 1 tablespoon of the oil into the cake pan and put in the oven to heat.

Meanwhile, heat the remaining oil in a non-stick frying pan/skillet, add the sliced potatoes and onion and cook over a medium heat for about 15 minutes, turning occasionally, until almost tender. Add the mushrooms and pepper and cook for 5 minutes.

Break the eggs into a large bowl and whisk briefly with a fork. Add the oregano and season with salt and pepper. Remove the vegetables from the pan with a slotted spoon, and add to the eggs. Stir gently.

Transfer to the preheated cake pan, return to the oven and cook for 15–20 minutes or until the egg is just set in the centre.

Turn the tortilla out onto a board and cut into small squares. Serve hot or at room temperature.

Spinach & Salt Cod Tortilla

Salt cod with spinach makes a wonderful combination of flavours and textures, and the potatoes make this tortilla quite hearty.

100 g/3½ oz. boneless salt cod, cut into cubes

100 ml/scant ½ cup olive oil

250 g/9 oz. potatoes, peeled and thinly sliced

1 small onion, finely chopped

6 eggs

125 g/4 oz. cooked spinach (from 250 g/9 oz. uncooked)

freshly ground black pepper

a 24-cm/9½-inch heavy non-stick frying pan/skillet (measure the base, not the top)

Serves 4

To prepare the salt cod, soak it in a bowl of cold water for 24 hours, changing the water every 4–5 hours. Just before you are ready to use it, drain well.

Heat 75 ml/5 tablespoons of the oil in a frying pan/skillet, add the potatoes and cook over a medium heat for 5 minutes. Add the onion and cook for 10 minutes or until the potatoes are almost tender, lifting and turning occasionally.

Lightly beat the eggs in a bowl with some black pepper. It usually isn't necessary to add salt because the fish is already salty. Mix in the spinach and flaked fish.

Pour the mixture into the frying pan, moving it with a spatula so that it flows under and over the potatoes. Cook until set on the bottom – shake the pan as it cooks and loosen the sides a little with a spatula.

Put a plate on top of the pan, turn it upside down, then slide the tortilla onto the plate. Put the remaining oil in the pan. When hot, slide the tortilla back in, cooked-side up. Cook for another 2–3 minutes until lightly browned on the other side.

Cut into squares and serve hot or at room temperature.

Artichoke & Ham Tortilla

This tortilla is topped with Serrano ham and finished under the grill/broiler. You can add a few slices of goat's cheese on the top, too.

3 tbsp olive oil

3 potatoes, about 350 g/12 oz., peeled and cubed

1 Spanish onion, chopped

5 large (US extra large) eggs

400 g/2 cups canned artichoke hearts in water, well drained and halved

2 tbsp fresh thyme leaves

100 g/3½ oz. thinly sliced Serrano ham, torn into strips

6–8 slices of goat's cheese log with rind, about 125 g/4 oz. (optional)

salt and freshly ground black pepper

a 24-cm/9½-inch heavy non-stick frying pan/skillet (measure the base, not the top)

Serves 4

Heat 2 tablespoons of the oil in the frying pan/skillet. Add the potatoes and cook over a medium heat for 5 minutes. Then add the onion and cook for a further 10 minutes, lifting and turning occasionally, until just tender. The potatoes and onion should not brown very much.

Meanwhile, break the eggs into a large bowl, season with salt and pepper and whisk briefly with a fork.

Add the artichokes, thyme and about three-quarters of the Serrano ham to the eggs. Next add the potatoes and onion and stir gently.

Heat the remaining oil in the frying pan. Add the tortilla mixture, spreading it out evenly in the pan. Cook over a medium–low heat for about 6 minutes, then top with the remaining ham. Cook for a further 4–5 minutes or until the bottom is golden brown and the top almost set.

Add the goat's cheese, if using, and slide under a preheated grill/broiler for 2–3 minutes, just to brown the top. Serve hot or warm, cut into wedges.

Baked Mushrooms with Manchego Béchamel

Look for mushrooms that will be two to three small mouthfuls in size – wild field mushrooms or the large portobello mushrooms are ideal.

2 tsp butter

2 tsp plain/all-purpose flour

125 ml/½ cup milk

50 g/1¾ oz. Manchego cheese, finely grated

12 wide, flat field mushrooms

¼ tsp oak-smoked sweet Spanish paprika

FENNEL SALAD

1 small fennel bulb

a handful of fresh flat-leaf parsley leaves

2 tsp olive oil

2 tsp freshly squeezed lemon juice

salt and freshly ground black pepper

Serves 4

Put the butter in a small saucepan and cook over a high heat until it is melted. Add the flour to the pan and stir quickly to form a thick paste. Remove from the heat and add a little of the milk, stirring continuously, until thick and smooth. Return the pan to a medium heat and add the remaining milk, whisking continuously until all the milk is incorporated and the mixture is smooth and thick. Add the cheese and stir until melted. Remove from the heat and let cool.

Preheat the oven to 220°C (425°F) Gas 7.

Remove the stalks from the mushrooms and sit the mushrooms in a small baking dish, gill-side up. Spoon the cheese sauce into the caps and sprinkle the paprika over the top.

Cook in the preheated oven for 20 minutes until the mushrooms are soft and the sauce is bubbling.

While the mushrooms are cooking, slice the fennel bulb as finely as possible, chop the fronds and put in a bowl with the parsley, oil and lemon juice. Toss the salad to combine, season to taste and serve with the warm mushrooms.

Alioli

Alioli is the garlic-laden version of the Spanish mayonnaise, *mahonesa*, thought to have originated in Mahon, the capital of the island of Menorca. To help stop it separating, have all the ingredients at room temperature, perhaps slightly warming the oil first. It is the essential accompaniment to many tapas dishes.

4–6 garlic cloves, crushed

1 egg

1 egg yolk

1 tsp freshly squeezed lemon juice

500 ml/2 cups light olive oil (not extra virgin)

salt and freshly ground black pepper

Serves 4

Put the garlic, egg, egg yolk and lemon juice in a food processor. Blend until pale yellow.

Keeping the motor running, slowly pour in the oil, a little at a time. Blend well until thick and silky, then add salt and pepper to taste.

Serve at room temperature.

Serving suggestion: Alioli with potatoes: Put 500 g/ 1 lb. 2 oz. unpeeled new potatoes in a saucepan, cover with cold water, add a pinch of salt and boil until tender. Drain and let cool. Slip off the skins, cut the potatoes into bite-sized pieces, then serve with the alioli for dipping.

Cheese Balls

2 tbsp plain/all-purpose flour

2 tbsp milk

½ tsp oak-smoked sweet Spanish paprika

1 egg

1 garlic clove, crushed

150 g/5¼ oz. Manchego cheese, finely grated

150 g/5¼ oz. soft goat's cheese, preferably Spanish

2 egg whites

1 tsp chopped fresh thyme leaves

1 tbsp Serrano ham, finely chopped

salt and ground white pepper

oil, for deep-frying

Serves 4

Manchego cheese is popular all over Spain. It is to the Spanish what Parmesan is to the Italians. The Manchego sheep's cheese and Spanish goat's cheese balance each other perfectly. This dish will be a real treat for your guests.

Put the flour and milk in a bowl and stir until smooth. Add the paprika, egg, garlic, both cheeses and a pinch of salt and white pepper. Mix well.

Put the egg whites in a bowl and whisk until stiff. Fold one-third into the flour mixture and mix well, then gently fold in the remaining egg whites, taking care not to lose all of the air. Sprinkle with the thyme and Serrano ham.

Fill a saucepan or deep-fryer one-third full of oil and heat to 195°C (380°F).

Using a teaspoon, run the spoon through the mixture, collecting an even amount of thyme and Serrano ham, and drop a heaped spoonful into the hot oil. Cook for 3 minutes or until the mixture is golden brown.

Drain on paper towels and serve immediately with wooden cocktail sticks/toothpicks.

Fried Cheese

Fried cheese, or *queso frito*, is best eaten hot, straight from the pan. It is one of the most popular tapas, perfect with manzanilla or fino sherry, or with Valdepeñas, a red wine from La Mancha.

275–300 g/9½–10½ oz. semi-cured Manchego cheese, 3 months old

2 tbsp plain/all-purpose flour

1 egg, beaten

150 g/2 cups lightly dried fine fresh white breadcrumbs

150 ml/⅔ cup olive oil

a pinch of oak-smoked sweet Spanish paprika

TO SERVE (OPTIONAL)
membrillo (quince paste)

mixed olives

Serves 6

Cut all the rind off the Manchego and cut the cheese into 1-cm/½-inch wedges.

Put the flour on a small plate, the beaten egg in a shallow dish and the breadcrumbs on another plate. Working in batches of six, dip each wedge of cheese first in the flour, then in the beaten egg and lastly in the breadcrumbs.

Heat half the oil in a non-stick frying pan/skillet over a medium heat, then fry the first batch for 45 seconds on each side until golden. Drain on paper towels.

Wipe out the pan (to remove any burned breadcrumbs) and fry the remaining batches in the same way.

Sprinkle with the paprika and serve with membrillo or olives, if using.

Note: Membrillo is a thick paste made from quinces, a golden fruit related to the apple and pear, available in autumn/fall. Quinces are cooked into desserts, jellies or jams, and into this sweetly smoky paste. Membrillo can also be served with a good Manchego cheese instead of dessert.

Aubergine Cheese Fritters

1 large aubergine/eggplant, about 350 g/12 oz.

150–200 g/5¼–7 oz. strong, meltable cheese, such as Cabrales or Cheddar

100 g/⅔ cup plain/all-purpose flour, seasoned with salt and pepper

2 medium (US large) eggs, well beaten with a fork

oil, for deep-frying

SALSA
2 medium vine-ripened tomatoes, chopped

60 ml/¼ cup chilli/chili oil (or olive oil mixed with ½ tsp Tabasco sauce)

4 tsp red wine vinegar or sherry vinegar

12 fresh basil leaves

salt and freshly ground black pepper

cocktail sticks/toothpicks

Serves 4

This tapas dish is served in Barcelona with the local rosé or red wine, well chilled.

Using a serrated knife, cut the aubergine crossways into 18–24 thin slices about 5 mm/¼ inch thick. Slice the cheese into pieces of the same thickness. Sandwich a piece of cheese between two pieces of aubergine. To keep the 'sandwiches' closed during cooking, push a cocktail stick/toothpick, at an angle, through each one.

Put the flour on a plate and pour the beaten eggs into a shallow dish.

Fill a saucepan or deep-fryer one-third full of oil and heat to 195°C (380°F).

Working in batches, dip the aubergine 'sandwiches' first into the flour, then into the beaten eggs, then in the flour again to coat. Slide them into the hot oil and fry for 2–3 minutes on the first side. Using tongs, turn and cook for 1–2 minutes on the other side until golden, with the cheese melting inside. Drain on paper towels while you coat and cook the rest.

To make the salsa, put the tomatoes, chilli oil, vinegar, basil leaves, and a pinch of salt and pepper in a food processor. Pulse in brief bursts to a coarse mixture.

Serve the fritters hot with a trickle of the salsa, or with a little pot of salsa as a dip.

Chapter 2

MEAT & POULTRY

Chorizo In Red Wine

Chorizo comes in many different varieties. You can get smoked or unsmoked, fresh or cured. Spicy fresh chorizo, the size of regular breakfast sausages, works well in this recipe. Large quantities of paprika give the dish a rich colour and a pungent flavour. Each region of Spain has its own version of this classic tapas dish – this one is simple and delicious.

1 tbsp olive oil

300 g/10½ oz. small, spicy fresh chorizo sausages, cut into 1-cm/½-inch slices

100 ml/scant ½ cup red wine

Serves 4

Put the oil in a heavy-based frying pan/skillet and heat until smoking.

Add the chorizo and cook for 1 minute. Reduce the heat, add the wine and cook for 5 minutes.

Transfer to a serving dish and set aside for a few minutes to develop the flavours.

Chorizo Potato Salad

This flavour-packed salad combines jarred artichoke hearts, pimento-stuffed olives and preserved piquillo peppers. Serve this tapas dish with a glass of chilled white wine or fino sherry.

500 g/1 lb. 2 oz. waxy potatoes, peeled

2 tbsp dry white wine

1 fresh chorizo, thinly sliced

2 tbsp extra virgin olive oil

75 g/2¾ oz. jarred, marinated artichoke hearts, chopped

8 pimento-stuffed olives, sliced

2 preserved piquillo peppers, chopped

2 tbsp chopped fresh flat-leaf parsley

salt and freshly ground black pepper

Serves 4

Cook the potatoes in a saucepan of boiling, salted water until tender, then drain. Place the hot potatoes in a bowl, pour over the white wine and set aside.

In a small frying pan/skillet, fry the chorizo over a low heat in its own fat, stirring often, until cooked through and lightly browned.

Slice the potatoes and toss with the olive oil in a bowl. Add the fried chorizo, artichoke hearts, olives, peppers and parsley, tossing well so that the potatoes take on the colour of the chorizo. Season with salt and freshly ground black pepper.

Serve at room temperature.

Catalan Chickpeas & Chorizo

This delicious, warm salad relies on just a handful of ingredients. With such a wonderful combination of flavours, you would never guess that it has a cooking time of just five minutes. You can forgo the pine nuts, but they do add a lovely bite to this tapas dish.

3 tbsp extra virgin olive oil

1 red onion, sliced

2 garlic cloves, chopped

200 g/7 oz. cured chorizo, sliced

2 bay leaves, bruised

2 tbsp pine nuts, toasted in a dry frying pan/skillet (optional)

400 g/2 cups canned chickpeas/garbanzo beans, drained, reserving 2 tbsp of their liquid

1 small tomato, finely chopped

freshly ground black pepper

Serves 4

Heat the oil in a frying pan/skillet, add the onion, garlic, chorizo and bay leaves and sauté over a gentle heat for 5 minutes, or until softened but not browned.

Stir in the toasted pine nuts, if using, and chickpeas with the reserved 2 tablespoons liquid. Heat until the flavours are combined, mashing a little with a fork.

Sprinkle with the finely chopped tomato and some ground black pepper.

Serve hot, warm or cool, but never chilled.

Artichokes with Serrano Ham

For this recipe, you need the tiny, often purplish-green variety of artichoke, available in early summer before it develops the hairy choke above the heart. Serve this tapas dish with a crisp sherry such as a manzanilla, from the seaside town of Sanlúcar de Barrameda.

1 lemon, halved

750 g/1½ lb. very small artichokes

4 tbsp extra virgin olive oil

8 slices of Serrano ham, chopped

3 tbsp chopped fresh flat-leaf parsley

salt and freshly ground black pepper

Serves 4

Fill a saucepan with water and squeeze in the juice from the halved lemon. Add the squeezed halves of lemon and some salt.

Trim the stalk of each artichoke to 1 cm/½ inch, then trim off all the outer leaves until you reach the tender inner leaves. Cut each artichoke in half lengthways. As you prepare them, add them to the pan of lemon water to stop them turning brown.

Bring to the boil, then lower the heat and simmer for about 7 minutes until just tender. Drain and dry.

Heat the oil in a frying pan/skillet, add the artichokes cut-side down and sauté for 5 minutes. Turn them over and sauté the other side for a further 2 minutes.

Add the Serrano ham and cook for a further 4 minutes until crisp and golden.

Sprinkle with the parsley and some ground black pepper, and serve.

Migas with Serrano Ham

200 g/7 oz. 2-day-old
dry country bread, crusts
removed

125 ml/½ cup extra virgin
olive oil

100 g/3½ oz. Serrano ham,
cut into 5-mm/¼-inch
pieces, or bacon lardons

3 garlic cloves, bruised with
the back of a knife

1 fat dried red chilli/chile,
such as ñora or ancho,
deseeded and finely chopped

salt

Serves 4

Migas, meaning 'breadcrumbs' in Spanish, are a national treasure. They are simply bread sprinkled with salted water, then fried in olive oil. There are countless regional variations of this tapas classic; these are from Extremadura and they go very well with Cava.

Cut the bread into fingers, spread it out on a kitchen towel, then sprinkle lightly with water and a little salt. Wrap up in the towel and leave for 2 hours.

After 2 hours, unwrap the bread and break it into chunky pieces.

Heat 2 teaspoons of the oil in a frying pan/skillet, add the ham and fry until crisp. Drain on paper towels.

Wipe the pan clean and heat the remaining oil. Add the garlic, sauté until golden, then remove and discard. Add all the breadcrumbs at once and stir-fry until evenly golden. Stir in the chilli and Serrano ham.

Serve very hot. This can be eaten with your fingers or using a small spoon.

Ham & Mushroom Croquettes

20 g/¾ oz. assorted dried mushrooms (such as porcini, morels, girolles, trompettes), soaked for 1 hour

25 g/2 tbsp butter

2 tbsp olive oil

1 leek, finely chopped

50 g/1¾ oz. Ibérico or air-dried ham, finely diced

70 g/generous ½ cup plain/all-purpose flour, plus extra for coating

350 ml/1½ cups milk

freshly grated nutmeg

3 medium (US large) eggs, beaten

100 g/1¼ cups fine dried breadcrumbs or matzo meal, for coating

sunflower or vegetable oil, for deep-frying

salt and freshly ground black pepper

Serves 6

Freshly fried croquettes are a real treat.

Strain the soaked mushrooms, reserving 3 tablespoons soaking water, and finely chop the mushrooms.

In a large pan, heat the butter and oil until melted. Add the leek and fry over a low–medium heat for 1 minute until softened. Add the ham and fry for 1 minute. Add the flour and cook the paste, stirring, for 5 minutes.

In a separate pan, heat the milk and reserved soaking water. Gradually add the hot liquid to the paste, mixing continuously. Add the mushrooms. Stir over a low heat until thickened. Season with salt, pepper and nutmeg.

Transfer to a shallow dish, cool, cover with clingfilm/plastic wrap and chill for 2 hours or overnight.

Put the flour for coating on a plate, beaten eggs in a shallow bowl and dried breadcrumbs on a plate. Using floured hands and working quickly, shape the chilled mixture into walnut-sized balls, rolling them on the palm of your hand. Dip each croquette first in the flour, then in the egg, then finally breadcrumbs. Place on a tray and chill in the fridge for 30 minutes.

Heat the oil for deep-frying in a pan to 185°C (365°F).

Deep-fry the croquettes in batches for 3–5 minutes, until golden on all sides. Remove with a slotted spoon and drain on paper towels. Serve at once.

Chicken with Garlic

This flavoursome dish finds its way onto almost every tapas menu in Spain and varies only slightly. It's so common, yet so simple to make. If you're unable to get hold of Brandy de Jerez, substitute it for Cognac or Armagnac.

8 chicken wings

1 tsp oak-smoked sweet Spanish paprika

1 tbsp lemon juice

2 tbsp olive oil

6 garlic cloves, coarsely crushed

150 ml/⅔ cup Brandy de Jerez

salt and freshly ground black pepper

Serves 4

Put the chicken wings in a non-reactive bowl, then rub the paprika evenly over the skin. Add the lemon juice, cover and let marinate in the refrigerator for 2 hours.

Heat the oil in a heavy-based frying pan/skillet until smoking, add the chicken and brown it on all sides.

Reduce the heat, add the garlic and cook for a further 2 minutes.

Add the brandy, tilt the pan to catch the flame and burn off the alcohol until the flames subside. Cover with a lid and simmer for 10 minutes.

Season to taste with salt and pepper, then serve.

Lamb with Lemon

This recipe is popular in Aragón and Murcia in central Spain, where meat-based tapas are preferred. The use of pineapple for tenderizing meat is a technique found in south-east Asia. It perhaps arrived in Spain from the former Spanish colony of the Philippines. Serve this dish with a good Rioja.

250 g/9 oz. lean lamb, such as the neck or loin

225 g/8 oz. canned pineapple slices, drained

10 cloves

1 lemon, halved

5 garlic cloves, peeled

2 tbsp olive oil

a sprig of fresh rosemary

½ small onion, finely chopped

a pinch of oak-smoked sweet Spanish paprika

Serves 4

Cut the lamb into 2-cm/¾-inch cubes. Put them in a bowl, cover with the pineapple slices and let marinate overnight, covered, in the refrigerator.

Preheat the oven to 150°C (300°F) Gas 2.

Stick the cloves into the lemon and put it in a roasting dish. Add the garlic, oil and rosemary. Remove the pineapple from the lamb and rub in the onion and paprika. Add the lamb to the roasting dish and cook in the oven for 15 minutes.

Take out of the oven, cover with foil and set aside for 10 minutes before serving.

150 g/5¼ oz. minced/ground pork

150 g/5¼ oz. minced/ground veal

1 tsp lemon juice

½ small onion, chopped

2 garlic cloves, crushed

2 tbsp chopped fresh flat-leaf parsley, plus extra to serve

½ tsp grated nutmeg

½ tsp ground cloves

30 g/¼ cup breadcrumbs

1 egg

1 tsp single/light cream

plain/all-purpose flour, to dust

2 tbsp olive oil

salt and ground white pepper

TOMATO SAUCE

125 ml/½ cup white wine

400 g/14 oz. canned chopped tomatoes

½ small onion, chopped

2 garlic cloves, crushed

½ tsp oak-smoked sweet Spanish paprika

1 fresh bay leaf

Serves 4

Meatballs with Spiced Tomato Sauce

These meatballs, or *albóndigas*, are a classic tapas dish and most deserving of their popularity. For a popular variation, serve with alioli (see page 24) and lemon rather than the tomato sauce, if you like.

To make the meatballs, put the pork and veal in a bowl, then add the lemon juice, onion, garlic, parsley, nutmeg, cloves, breadcrumbs, egg, cream, salt and pepper. Mix well, then roll into walnut-sized balls. Dust with flour.

Heat the oil in a flameproof casserole until smoking, add the meatballs and sauté until browned on all sides.

Reduce the heat to low. Add the wine, tomatoes, onion, garlic, paprika, bay leaf and 100 ml/scant ½ cup water. Cover and simmer for 1 hour. The mixture should be quite liquid, so add extra water if necessary.

Serve warm, sprinkled with extra chopped parsley.

Spicy Moorish Kebabs

This recipe is from Andalusia, where you see it in almost every tapas bar. The region is renowned for simple food, so this is a quick, easy recipe that leaves more time for other things, like socializing with guests.

2 tbsp olive oil

2 garlic cloves, crushed

1 dried red chilli/chile, crushed

1 tsp ground cumin

1 tsp ground fennel

1 tsp oak-smoked sweet Spanish paprika

freshly squeezed juice of 1 lemon

2 tbsp chopped fresh flat-leaf parsley

1 tbsp dry sherry

500 g/1 lb. 2 oz. pork tenderloin

metal kebab skewers or bamboo skewers soaked in water for 30 minutes

Serves 4

Put the oil, garlic, chilli, cumin, fennel, paprika, lemon juice, parsley and sherry in a bowl and mix well.

Cut the pork into 2-cm/¾-inch cubes and add to the bowl. Cover and chill overnight in the refrigerator.

When ready to cook, preheat a grill/broiler until hot.

Thread the pork onto the skewers and grill/broil for 10 minutes, turning often, taking care not to overcook the meat.

Remove from the heat and set aside to rest for about 10 minutes before serving warm.

Hot Sandwiches

Serve these tapas sandwiches, *emparedados calientes*, on a bamboo skewer with bowls of olives and Padrón peppers (see page 109).

8 slices of Serrano ham

12 thin slices of cured chorizo

8 slices of 3-day-old bread, crusts removed

2 tbsp grated Manchego cheese

4 medium (US large) eggs, beaten

90 ml/scant ½ cup extra virgin olive oil

salt and freshly ground black pepper

bamboo skewers

Serves 4

Divide the Serrano ham and chorizo between 4 slices of the bread. Grind over some black pepper and sprinkle the grated cheese on top of the chorizo, keeping it to the centre of the slices. Top with the remaining slices of bread and press down firmly.

Put the beaten eggs in a flat dish, large enough to take 2 sandwiches at a time and season with salt and black pepper. Dip the sandwiches in the mixture.

Heat half the oil in a non-stick frying pan/skillet large enough to take 2 sandwiches at a time. Sauté over a medium heat for about 3–3½ minutes on each side until crisp and golden. Repeat with the remaining oil and sandwiches.

Cut into triangles, thread onto bamboo skewers and serve while hot.

Chapter 3

FISH & SEAFOOD

Baked Sardines

75 ml/⅓ cup extra virgin olive oil

1 red (bell) pepper, halved, deseeded and finely chopped

2 onions, finely chopped

3 garlic cloves, crushed

2 large tomatoes, skinned, deseeded and cut into 2.5-cm/1-inch cubes

1 tsp hot paprika

a pinch of saffron threads, soaked in 1 tbsp water

¼ tsp ground cumin

2 bay leaves

2 tbsp chopped fresh flat-leaf parsley, plus extra to serve

9–12 fresh sardine fillets (depending on the size of the dish)

salt and freshly ground black pepper

Serves 4–6

A mixture of very finely chopped vegetables forms the base of this dish. It can be served either very hot straight from the oven or left until cold, which is perfect in summer. In true Spanish style, serve it with bread to mop up the juices.

Heat 3 tablespoons of the oil in a frying pan/skillet, add the red pepper, onions and garlic and cook gently for 8–10 minutes until softened but not coloured.

Add the tomatoes, paprika, saffron and its soaking water, cumin and bay leaves and cook for a further 5–8 minutes (add a little water if the mixture sticks to the pan) until completely cooked. Season with salt and pepper and fold in the parsley.

Preheat the oven to 190°C (375°F) Gas 5.

Put the sardine fillets on a plate, skin-side down, and sprinkle with a little salt and pepper.

Arrange one-third of the fillets, skin-side up, in an ovenproof dish and cover with one-third of the cooked mixture. Repeat twice more – when adding the last layer, let the silver sardine skin peek through. Add a little more pepper and spoon over the rest of the oil.

Bake in a preheated oven for 15–20 minutes until sizzling. Sprinkle with parsley leaves, then serve.

Salt Cod Balls

Dried salt cod, known as *bacalao*, can be found in specialist shops. You could substitute it with fresh fish and halve the cooking time.

125 g/4 oz. boneless salt cod

300 g/10½ oz. potatoes

1 bay leaf

1 garlic clove, crushed

1 tbsp chopped fresh flat-leaf parsley

1 medium (US large) egg

plain/all-purpose flour, for coating

ground white pepper

oil, for deep-frying

Alioli, to serve (see page 24)

Serves 4

To prepare the salt cod, soak it in cold water for 24 hours, changing the water every 4–5 hours. Just before you are ready to use it, drain well.

Preheat the oven to 200°C (400°F) Gas 6.

Prick the potatoes, arrange in a roasting pan, then bake for 1 hour until soft. Scoop the flesh out of the skins into a bowl and mash.

Put the cod in a pan, cover with water, add the bay leaf, bring to the boil and simmer for 30 minutes. Remove from the heat and let cool. Discard the skin and flake the flesh into a bowl, removing the bones. Add the flesh to the mashed potatoes and stir in the garlic, parsley, pepper and 2 tablespoons of the cod cooking liquid. Roll into walnut-sized balls. Put in a bowl, cover with clingfilm/plastic wrap and chill for 2–3 hours.

Crack the egg into a bowl, add 1 tablespoon water and beat lightly. Put the flour on a plate. Dip the cod balls in the beaten egg, then roll in the flour.

Fill a saucepan or deep-fryer one-third full of oil and heat to 195°C (380°F).

Cook the balls, in batches if necessary, for 3 minutes, or until golden brown. Remove with a slotted spoon and drain on paper towels. Serve hot with Alioli.

Peppers Stuffed with Salt Cod

Piquillo peppers are grown in the Navarra region in the north of Spain. The word *piquillo* in Spanish means 'little beak'. These peppers are slightly sour and very small, so perfect for tapas. If you cannot get hold of any, use jarred roasted red peppers.

150 g/5¼ oz. salt cod

200 ml/scant 1 cup milk

1 small onion, finely sliced

2 bay leaves

a sprig of fresh flat leaf parsley

25 g/2 tbsp unsalted butter

2 tbsp plain/all-purpose flour

8 canned piquillo peppers, drained

salt and ground white pepper

Serves 4

To prepare the salt cod, soak it in cold water for 24 hours, changing the water every 4–5 hours. Just before you are ready to use it, drain well.

Put the milk in a saucepan, then add the onion, bay leaves and parsley. Heat almost to boiling, then remove from the heat and let cool before straining.

Melt the butter in a saucepan, then stir in the flour and cook for 1 minute. Slowly stir in the strained milk. Cook over a medium heat for 3 minutes, or until the mixture is thick. Season with salt and pepper and let cool.

Put the cod in a saucepan and cover with water. Bring to the boil, then simmer for 20 minutes. Remove the cod and pat dry with paper towels. Remove the skin and flake the flesh into a bowl, making sure to remove all the bones. Pour in the white sauce and mix well.

Stuff into the cavity of the peppers, then refrigerate for 2 hours or overnight.

Preheat the oven to 150°C (300°F) Gas 2.

Transfer the peppers to an ovenproof dish and cook in the oven for 15 minutes. Serve in a bowl.

Marinated Anchovies

People tend to be intimidated by these little fish, but have no fear, they are easy to prepare and taste simply divine. They are popular all over Spain and appear as simple tapas (*boquerones en vinegre*) throughout the country.

150 g/5¼ oz. fresh anchovies

100 ml/scant ½ cup good-quality white wine vinegar

3 garlic cloves, sliced

1 tbsp chopped fresh flat-leaf parsley

100 ml/scant ½ cup olive oil

Serves 4

To clean the anchovies, run your finger down the belly side and open up the fish. Pull the spine from the head and separate it from the flesh. Remove the head. Wash the fish and let dry on paper towels.

Put the anchovies in a plastic container and pour in the vinegar. Cover and let marinate in the refrigerator overnight.

The next day, rinse the anchovies and put them in a serving dish with the garlic, parsley and olive oil. Cover and chill overnight.

To serve, return to room temperature, or you can keep the anchovies in the refrigerator to eat another day.

Note: If fresh anchovies are unavailable, use any small fish you can find. Aim for ones that are around 5–7.5 cm/2–3 inches long.

Marinated Sardines

Here the fish is 'cooked' in vinegar, which is perfect with the healthy, sweet oiliness of sardines.

8 fresh sardines, about 500 g/1 lb. 2 oz.

2 tbsp olive oil

50 ml/3½ tbsp good-quality white wine vinegar

100 ml/scant ½ cup dry white wine

2 garlic cloves, sliced

4 fresh bay leaves

1 tsp fennel seeds, lightly crushed

½ tsp dried chilli/hot red pepper flakes

2 sprigs of fresh thyme

4 slices of lemon

Serves 4

To clean the sardines, wash them in cold water and scrape off any scales. Put each fish on a board, take off the head, run a knife from the head halfway down the belly side and scrape out the insides. Wash the fish and let dry on a paper towel. Run your thumb down the inside of the fish along the bone and squash the fillets flat. Gently pull the backbone away from the flesh towards the tail. Cut with scissors.

Heat the oil in a heavy-based frying pan/skillet, add the vinegar, wine, garlic, bay leaves, fennel, chilli flakes and thyme, then bring to the boil for 3 minutes. Add the sardines, skin-side up, then remove from the heat.

Arrange the sardines in a single layer in a plastic or ceramic dish, put the slices of lemon on top, then pour over the liquid and cover with clingfilm/plastic wrap. Let marinate in the refrigerator overnight.

Serve at room temperature or leave in the refrigerator to eat another day.

Marinated Octopus

Some people avoid cooking octopus as it can be tough, but it makes a delicious small plate. Tapping the octopus against a hard surface will tenderize it (or buy it frozen, as freezing also helps tenderize it).

500 g/1 lb. 2 oz. octopus

3 tbsp olive oil

2 tbsp red wine vinegar

2 garlic cloves, crushed

½ tsp oak-smoked sweet Spanish paprika

½ tsp dried chilli/hot red pepper flakes

1 tbsp capers, chopped

3 tbsp chopped fresh flat-leaf parsley

freshly squeezed juice of 1 lemon

salt and freshly ground black pepper

Serves 4

If the octopus hasn't been frozen, you should throw it against a hard surface ten times to tenderize the meat. Put it on a chopping board, cut off the head just below the eyes and discard, then squeeze out and discard the beak, which is in the centre of the tentacles. Rinse out the body.

Bring a large saucepan of water to the boil, then blanch the octopus for 30 seconds and repeat 4–5 times. Return the octopus to the saucepan, cover with a lid and simmer for 1 hour.

Test the octopus for tenderness – if it's still tough, continue cooking for another 20 minutes. Remove from the heat, let cool, then drain. Cut the tentacles into 2.5-cm/1-inch lengths and the body into bite-sized pieces.

Heat the oil in a frying pan/skillet, add the vinegar, garlic, paprika, chilli flakes, capers, 2 tablespoons of the parsley and the octopus. Bring to the boil, then simmer for 3 minutes. Transfer to a plastic or ceramic dish and let cool. Season, then cover and let marinate in the refrigerator overnight.

Serve at room temperature with the lemon juice squeezed over and parsley sprinkled on top.

Spanish Clams with Serrano Ham

Mediterranean live clams usually go straight into the cooking pot with oil and garlic. However, because Spanish cured hams are so exceptional, adding even a little ham will season and enliven the clams. *Mar i montaña*, meaning 'sea and mountains', is the combination of meat with fish or seafood, and it is a typically Catalan cooking idea. The cooking time for this recipe is just a few minutes, meaning that this tapas dish is ready in a flash.

2 tbsp extra virgin olive oil

500 g/1 lb. 2 oz. small fresh clams, or frozen uncooked clams

50 g/1¾ oz. Serrano ham, cut into thin strips

1 small green chilli/chile, deseeded and chopped

2 garlic cloves, sliced

60 ml/¼ cup white wine or cider

2 tbsp chopped spring onion/scallion tops, chives or flat-leaf parsley

Serves 4

Put the oil, clams, Serrano ham, chilli and garlic in a saucepan and stir over a high heat.

When the Serrano ham is cooked and the clams begin to open, add the wine, cover the saucepan and shake it to mix the ingredients.

Cook on high for a further 2–3 minutes, or until the clams have opened and are cooked (discard any that don't open).

Sprinkle with the chopped spring onion tops. Cover again for 1 minute, then ladle into shallow soup bowls.

Squid with Alioli

This simple dish will bring a lovely taste of the Spanish coast to your tapas selection. The squid may well be deep-fried, but they taste lovely and light, with the alioli making the perfect accompaniment as a dipping sauce.

100–200 g/²/₃–1¹/₃ cups semolina flour

½–1 tsp salt

½–1 tsp dried oregano or marjoram leaves, crumbled

8 squid or cuttlefish tubes, sliced into 1-cm/½-inch rounds

extra virgin olive oil, for deep-frying

½ lemon, to serve

Alioli, to serve (see page 24)

Serves 4

Put the semolina flour, salt and oregano in a bowl. Pat the squid rings dry with paper towels and toss them in the flour mixture until well coated.

Fill a deep frying pan/skillet or an electric deep-fryer one-third full with oil and heat to 195°C (380°F).

Fry the prepared squid in the hot oil in batches. Cook for 30–45 seconds, the minimum time it takes to set the seafood to firm whiteness and make the coating crisp. Remove, drain and keep hot. Continue until all of the squid are cooked.

Serve a pile of squid rings on each plate, with the lemon half for squeezing and a large spoonful of alioli.

Stuffed Squid

75 ml/⅓ cup extra virgin olive oil

1 onion, finely chopped

16 cleaned baby squid with tentacles, about 7.5 cm/ 3 inches long

50 g/1¾ oz. cured chorizo, finely chopped

½ tsp dried chilli/hot red pepper flakes

70 g/½ cup pine nuts

2 garlic cloves, finely chopped

2 tbsp chopped fresh flat-leaf parsley, plus extra to serve

175 ml/¾ cup fresh breadcrumbs

TOMATO SAUCE
2 tbsp extra virgin olive oil

1 onion, finely chopped

1 garlic clove, finely chopped

½ tsp sugar

6 tomatoes, skinned, deseeded and finely chopped, reserving any juices

wooden cocktail sticks/toothpicks

Serves 4

Use small squid if you can get hold of them as they are more likely to be tender.

Preheat the oven to 190°C (375°F) Gas 5.

Heat 3 tablespoons of the oil in a frying pan/skillet, add the onion and sauté until soft and pale golden.

Finely chop the tentacles and add to the pan and sauté until pale. Next add the chorizo and sauté until the fat runs out into the onion. Stir in the chilli flakes.

Toast the pine nuts in a dry frying pan for a minute or so until golden. Take care because they will burn easily. Transfer to a plate to cool.

Pulse the garlic, parsley, breadcrumbs and half the pine nuts in a processor until fine. Add to the pan. Let cool.

To make the tomato sauce, heat the oil in a saucepan, add the onion and garlic and sauté until pale golden. Increase the heat, add the sugar and tomatoes with their juices, then simmer for a few minutes.

Stuff the squid with the cold chorizo mixture and close with a cocktail stick.

Heat the remaining oil in a frying pan, add the stuffed squid and sauté on both sides until pale golden, about 2 minutes on each side. Add to the sauce and cook in the preheated oven for 15 minutes.

Remove from the oven, sprinkle with the extra parsley and remaining toasted pine nuts and serve.

Mussels with Fennel Alioli

Although you can buy ready-cooked and flavoured, vacuum-packed mussels, it's much better to buy them fresh and clean them yourself.

1 kg/2¼ lbs. live mussels

2 small fennel bulbs, with feathery tops intact and reserved for the alioli

1 tbsp olive oil

1 tbsp butter

1 garlic clove, finely chopped

1 small onion or 2 shallots, finely chopped

125 ml/½ cup dry white wine

250 ml/1 cup fish stock/broth

2 ripe tomatoes, diced

a handful of fresh flat-leaf parsley, roughly chopped

FENNEL ALIOLI
reserved fennel tops
(see above)

185 ml/⅔ cup good-quality mayonnaise

3 garlic cloves, crushed

Serves 4

To clean the mussels, scrub them in cold water and pull off the beards. Tap them against a work surface and discard any mussels that don't close. Drain in a colander and set aside until they are needed.

To make the fennel alioli, finely chop the feathery tops of the fennel and combine in a small bowl with the mayonnaise and garlic. Cover and chill until needed.

Finely chop the fennel bulbs. Heat the oil and butter in a large saucepan set over a medium heat and gently cook the garlic, onion and fennel for about 10 minutes until the fennel has softened.

Add the wine, stock and tomatoes and bring to the boil. Cook for 5 minutes. Add the mussels, cover tightly with a lid and cook for a further 5 minutes, shaking the pan occasionally, until the mussels have opened. Discard any that don't open. Add the parsley and stir.

Spoon the mussels into serving bowls and put an empty bowl on the table for discarded shells. Serve with the fennel alioli.

Garlic Prawns

This quick-to-cook classic tapas dish, made from a few simple ingredients including garlic and smoked Spanish paprika, is addictively moreish. It works well as part of a tapas feast, but do make sure you have plenty of bread on hand for soaking up the flavourful olive oil.

4 tbsp olive oil

2 garlic cloves, chopped

2 small dried red chillies/chiles, crumbled

450 g/1 lb. raw prawns/shrimp, peeled, deveined, rinsed and dried

1 tsp oak-smoked sweet Spanish paprika

1 tbsp finely chopped fresh flat-leaf parsley

salt

crusty bread, to serve

Serves 4

Heat the olive oil in a heavy-based frying pan/skillet. Add the chopped garlic and fry briefly, stirring, until fragrant. Add the crumbled chillies, mixing well, then add the prawns, mixing to coat them in the oil.

Fry the prawns briefly, stirring, until they turn opaque and pink on both sides, taking care not to over-cook them and dry them out. Season with salt, then add the Spanish paprika, mixing in.

Sprinkle with parsley and serve at once.

Prawns in Overcoats

This tapas dish goes perfectly with a glass of cold beer. It's a simple recipe and can be whipped up in no time at all. This method of deep-frying will make the batter crisp, while the prawns/shrimp remain tender and juicy inside. Cook them in small batches so as not to reduce the temperature of the oil.

300 g/10½ oz. uncooked prawns/shrimp, shell on

125 g/¾ cup plain/all-purpose flour

1 tsp baking powder

a pinch of salt

a pinch of oak-smoked sweet Spanish paprika

250 ml/1 cup beer

oil, for frying

lemon wedges, to serve

Serves 4

Peel the prawns, but leave the tail fins intact.

Sift the flour, baking powder, salt and paprika into a bowl, mix well, then pour in the beer. Let rest for a few minutes.

Fill a saucepan or deep-fryer one-third full of oil and heat to 195°C (380°F).

Dip the prawns in the batter and cook in the oil until golden brown. Drain on paper towels.

Serve with lemon wedges on the side for squeezing.

Crispy Paella Balls with Romesco Sauce

2 tbsp olive oil

4 garlic cloves, crushed

1 tomato, finely chopped

1 tsp oak-smoked sweet Spanish paprika

200 g/7 oz. cooked, peeled prawns/shrimp, finely chopped

200 g/generous 1 cup bomba, Calasparra or arborio rice

600 ml/2½ cups hot chicken stock

3 medium (US large) eggs

4–6 tbsp plain/all-purpose flour

100 g/1¼ cups dried breadcrumbs

salt and freshly ground black pepper

sunflower oil, for deep frying

Romesco Sauce, to serve (see page 88)

Makes 16

These deep-fried paella balls are lovely as tapas with the piquant romesco sauce.

Heat the oil in a 25-cm/10-in. paella pan (or shallow flameproof casserole) and fry the garlic over a low heat for 5 minutes until softened.

Add the tomato, paprika and a little salt and black pepper, and cook for 5 minutes.

Stir in the prawns, then the rice. Add the stock, bring to the boil and simmer gently for 20 minutes, until the rice is al dente and the stock absorbed. Let cool, then chill the paella for 1 hour.

Beat one of the eggs and work into the chilled rice until combined. Shape into 16 golf ball-sized balls.

Beat the two remaining eggs and place in a shallow dish. Put the flour in another dish and the breadcrumbs in a third. Dust each ball lightly with flour, dip into the egg and then coat with breadcrumbs.

Fill a saucepan or deep-fryer one-third full of oil and heat to 195°C (380°F).

Add the balls a few at a time and fry for 4–5 minutes, turning halfway through, until golden brown. Drain on paper towels and repeat with the remaining balls.

Serve with the Romesco Sauce.

Chapter 4

VEGETABLES

Patatas Bravas

300 g/10 ½ oz. waxy potatoes, peeled

2 tbsp olive oil

1 shallot, chopped

1 garlic clove, chopped

1 dried chilli/hot red pepper

1 tbsp sherry vinegar

400 g/14 oz. canned plum tomatoes

1 tsp hot smoked paprika/pimentón

salt and freshly ground black pepper

chopped fresh flat-leaf parsley, to garnish

Serves 4

Patatas bravas, fried potatoes in a spicy tomato sauce is perhaps one of the most popular and of course traditional Spanish tapas dishes. Waxy potatoes are a must, as is pimentón, the hot smoked Spanish paprika.

Boil the potatoes in salted boiling water until just tender; drain, cool and dice.

Meanwhile, prepare the spicy tomato sauce. Heat 1 tablespoon of the oil in a small, heavy-bottomed frying pan/skillet. Add the shallot and garlic and crumble in the dried chilli. Fry, stirring, for 1–2 minutes until fragrant. Add the sherry vinegar and continue to cook for 1 minute until syrupy.

Add the canned tomatoes and mix well. Season with salt, pepper and the smoked paprika. Turn up the heat and bring to the boil. Cook the sauce uncovered, stirring often to break down the tomatoes, for 10–15 minutes, until reduced and thickened.

In a separate large frying pan, heat the remaining olive oil. Add the cooled, diced potatoes and fry until golden brown on all sides, stirring often. Season with salt.

Pour the cooked tomato sauce over the potatoes, garnish with chopped parsley and serve hot or at room temperature.

Potato Wedges with Romesco Sauce

Warm potato wedges – with their mild nuttiness – are an excellent foil for tangy, flavourful romesco, a classic Spanish sauce.

600 g/1 lb. 5 oz. even-sized potatoes

4 tbsp extra virgin olive oil

salt

chopped fresh flat-leaf parsley, to garnish

ROMESCO SAUCE

1 tbsp each blanched almonds and blanched hazelnuts, roughly chopped

5 tbsp extra virgin olive oil

2 large garlic cloves, chopped

1 ripe tomato, diced

1 small slice of bread, about 25 g/1 oz., crusts removed

1 roasted red/bell pepper from a jar, about 100 g/3½ oz.

1 tbsp red wine vinegar

¼ tsp Espelette pepper (or cayenne pepper)

Serves 4

Preheat the oven to 200°C (400°F) Gas 6.

Peel the potatoes, halve each one lengthways and slice each half into four wedges, making eight wedges per potato. Toss the wedges with 1 tablespoon of the olive oil and season with salt. Place in a roasting pan and bake in the preheated oven for 40–50 minutes until tender and blotched golden brown.

Meanwhile, make the romesco sauce. Gently fry the almonds and hazelnuts in 2 tablespoons of the oil until golden, then remove with a slotted spoon. Add the garlic to the pan and fry for 5 minutes, until soft, then add the tomato and cook for a further 5 minutes.

Transfer the tomato mixture to a blender or food processor, add the nuts, bread and red pepper, and blend until smooth. Gradually whisk in the remaining oil and the vinegar to make a smooth sauce. Add the Espelette pepper and some salt to taste.

Serve the potato wedges warm from the oven with the romesco sauce on the side. Garnish with parsley.

Potato Fritters with Chorizo

These tasty little fritters require just a handful of low-cost ingredients. Serve this tapas dish very hot, with lots of napkins, cocktail sticks, a bowl of coarse sea salt and a copita or two of chilled manzanilla sherry.

500 g/1 lb. 2 oz. potatoes, peeled and cut lengthways into thick fingers

1 tbsp self-raising/self-rising flour

2 eggs, separated, plus 1 egg white

100 g/3½ oz. cooked chorizo, skinned and chopped into small pieces

salt and freshly ground black pepper

olive oil, for deep-frying

Serves 4–6

Boil the potatoes in a saucepan of salted water until soft, drain through a colander and cover with a cloth for about 5 minutes to let them dry out. Transfer to a bowl, mash in the flour and season with a little pepper. Mix in the egg yolks, then stir in the chorizo.

Put the egg whites in a separate bowl and whisk until soft peaks form. Fold into the mashed potatoes a little at a time.

Fill a saucepan or deep-fryer one-third full with oil. Heat to 195°C (380°F).

Preheat the oven to 180°C (350°F) Gas 4.

Working in batches of six, take heaped teaspoons of the mixture and lower into the hot oil. Fry each batch for 3 minutes until evenly golden, turning them over halfway through (if they brown too quickly they will not have a good texture in the centre). Keep the oil temperature constant. Drain on paper towels and keep warm in the preheated oven until you have cooked the remaining fritters.

Serve hot with cocktail sticks/toothpicks.

Pan Catalan

Simple pleasures are the best. This classic Spanish snack is a wonderful addition to any tapas menu.

10 slices rustic bread

1 garlic clove, peeled

2 ripe, juicy tomatoes (such as Globe), halved

extra virgin olive oil, to drizzle

salt

Makes 20

Begin by toasting the bread slices under a grill/broiler until lightly golden on one side only.

Rub the peeled garlic over the toasted side of each bread slice. Rub the tomatoes cut-side down over the bread in the same way.

Cut each slice in half, drizzle generously with oil and season with a touch of salt. Serve at once.

Gazpacho

Gazpacho is a light summer soup. It originated in the south of Spain, traditionally in Andalusia. For best results use ripe tomatoes and a good-quality olive oil – but most importantly serve gazpacho icy cold.

1 garlic clove

a pinch of coarse salt

1 slice white bread, crusts removed

4 ripe juicy tomatoes, skinned and deseeded

1 tbsp grated onion

¼ small cucumber, peeled and deseeded, plus extra to serve

1 tbsp Spanish red wine vinegar

2 tbsp olive oil

1 tsp sugar

freshly ground black pepper

Serves 4

Grind the garlic and coarse salt together using a mortar and pestle.

Put the bread in a saucer with a little water and let soak.

Put the garlic-salt mixture, soaked bread, tomatoes, onion, cucumber and vinegar in a blender and purée until smooth. Keeping the motor running, add the oil in a slow and steady stream. Add salt and pepper to taste, then add the sugar.

Pour the mixture through a sieve/strainer into a bowl adding more seasoning and vinegar if necessary. Chill in the refrigerator overnight.

Serve in small bowls or glasses with a little chopped cucumber on top.

Ajo Blanco

Also known as white gazpacho, *ajo blanco* is a classic Spanish cold soup. It is simply made from a few humble ingredients and has a delicate nutty flavour. Garnished, as is traditional, with fresh grapes or melon, it makes a visually appealing and extremely refreshing tapas dish.

100 g/3½ oz. slightly stale white bread, crusts trimmed, sliced

700 ml/3 cups cold water

200 g/1½ cups blanched almonds

2 garlic cloves, crushed

6 tbsp extra virgin olive oil, plus extra to serve

2 tbsp sherry vinegar

salt

a handful of white seedless grapes, halved, or small melon chunks

Serves 4

Soak the bread in the cold water for about 30 minutes until softened.

Finely grind the almonds in a food processor. Add the soaked bread and half the soaking water, reserving the remainder. Blitz until smooth. Add the crushed garlic, olive oil and sherry vinegar and blend together until smooth.

Add in enough of the remaining soaking water to give the soup a creamy texture. Season with salt. Cover and chill in the fridge for at least 2–3 hours.

Serve garnished with a drizzle of olive oil and grape halves or small chunks of melon.

Pinchos

Pinchos are little morsels that are usually eaten on an honesty system – you help yourself to the different varieties on display. Generally, they are eaten without a plate, and in some bars you are charged according to the number of cocktail sticks/toothpicks you've used.

2 tbsp olive oil

1 garlic clove, crushed

½ tsp dried chilli/hot red pepper flakes

leaves from 2 sprigs of fresh thyme, plus extra to serve

100 g/3½ oz. white asparagus, canned or from a jar

2 tbsp ground almonds

8 slices of white bread, lightly toasted and cut into circles

½ can pimientos, chopped

salt and freshly ground black pepper

Serves 4

Put the oil, garlic, chilli flakes and thyme in a saucepan, bring to the boil, then remove from the heat. Let cool, then strain.

Put the asparagus in a blender and pulse until smooth. Slowly add the strained oil and blend again. Mix in the ground almonds and salt and pepper to taste.

Spoon the asparagus mixture onto the toasted bread circles and top with the sliced pimiento. Add a few thyme leaves and serve.

Warm Marinated Olives

These delicious marinated olives go very well with some crusty bread and a fruity sangría. Tapas perfection.

100 g/3½ oz. large green olives

100 g/3½ oz. small black olives

250 ml/1 cup extra virgin olive oil

2 sprigs of fresh thyme

2 dried red chillies/chiles

1 bay leaf

2 thin slices of orange zest

crusty bread, to serve

Serves 6–8

Put the olives in a small, heatproof bowl and set aside.

Put the oil, thyme, chillies, bay leaf and orange zest in a small saucepan and set over a medium heat.

As soon as you hear the herbs starting to sizzle in the oil, remove the pan from the heat and pour the mixture over the olives. Let cool for 20 minutes.

Serve with some crusty bread for mopping up the oil.

Artichoke Hearts Marinated in Garlic

Artichokes are easier to cook than you might think. Just make sure you remove as many of the green leaves as possible because they can be tough. As you prepare them, put them in a bowl of cold water with a squeeze of lemon juice to stop them discolouring, and don't be afraid of overcooking them.

8 small artichokes

freshly squeezed juice of 1 lemon and grated zest of ½ unwaxed lemon

3 tbsp olive oil

6 garlic cloves, peeled

a sprig of fresh thyme

2 tbsp Spanish red wine vinegar

a sprig of fresh flat-leaf parsley

salt and ground white pepper

Serves 4

Cut off the artichoke stalks 1 cm/½ inch from the base. Trim off the outer leaves and, using a potato peeler, peel the outer sections and remove the green leaves. Cut off the tip and spoon out any furry bits from the middle section (this is called the choke). As you prepare them, put them in a bowl of cold water with the lemon juice.

Bring a pan of salted water to the boil, add the artichoke hearts and cook for 20 minutes until tender.

Meanwhile put the oil, garlic, thyme and lemon zest in a small saucepan and heat gently. Remove from the heat and leave to infuse.

Drain the artichokes, cut in half and dry on paper towels. Transfer to a bowl, then add the garlic oil, the vinegar and parsley and stir well. Sprinkle with salt and pepper, cover and let marinate in the refrigerator for 2–3 days.

Serve at room temperature.

Grilled Wild Asparagus

Asparagus served with alioli, coarse sea salt and sautéed sliced baby chorizos is a simple dish. True wild asparagus grows on the edges of wheatfields in spring and is called *trigueros* (after *trigo*, the Spanish word for 'wheat'). Sweet in flavour, it is a much paler green than our thin asparagus.

750 g/1½ lb. thin asparagus

3 tbsp olive oil

2 baby chorizos, sliced

salt and freshly ground black pepper

Alioli, to serve (see page 24)

Serves 4

Trim the asparagus and peel away the papery triangular bits from the stalk. Put the oil, salt and pepper in a shallow dish, add the asparagus and turn to coat.

Heat a ridged stove-top grill pan until smoking. Cook the asparagus, in batches, turning them over when |grill marks appear. They will take 1½–2½ minutes on each side.

Fry the sliced chorizos in a dry frying pan/skillet until crispy.

Serve while still hot with the alioli, some sea salt and the fried chorizos in small bowls.

Marinated Peppers

Marinated peppers are very simple but taste fantastic; for the best result, use small peppers. Serve on a slice of bread or toast, or go that bit further and serve the bread old-fashioned tapas-style on top of a glass of chilled sherry.

3 small red (bell) peppers

3 tbsp olive oil

60 ml/¼ cup sherry vinegar

a sprig of fresh thyme

a sprig of fresh rosemary

2 garlic cloves, sliced

½ tsp cayenne pepper

1 tbsp salted capers, rinsed and drained

1 tbsp chopped fresh flat-leaf parsley

salt and ground white pepper

thinly sliced bread, to serve

Serves 4

Grill the peppers slowly under a preheated grill/broiler until the skins are blistered and black. Transfer to a plastic bag, seal and let steam. When cool enough to handle, pull off the skins and remove the seeds and membranes. Put the peppers in a sieve/strainer set over a bowl to catch the juices and cut into 1-cm/½-inch strips.

Heat a heavy-based frying pan/skillet, then add the oil, vinegar, thyme, rosemary, garlic, cayenne pepper and the collected pepper juices. Cook over a low heat for 2 minutes. Add the peppers, capers, parsley and salt and pepper to taste. Cook, stirring, for 1 minute. Remove from the heat and let cool. Transfer to a bowl, cover and chill overnight.

When ready to eat, return to room temperature and serve on a thin slice of bread.

The marinated peppers can be kept in the refrigerator for up to a week.

Padrón Peppers

Padrón peppers can sometimes be hard to find, but stock up a little when you do as they keep surprisingly well in the fridge.

20 Padrón peppers

1 tbsp good olive oil

sea salt flakes

Serves 4–6

Wash the peppers and pat dry on paper towels, but do not destalk them.

Heat the oil in a frying pan/skillet over a medium heat and fry the peppers in small batches, turning frequently, until they begin to change colour and the skin starts to puff up. Remove from the pan and drain on paper towels.

Season with salt flakes and serve.

Note: Be warned! Although Padrón peppers are generally very mild, about 1 in 10 can have a spicy kick.

Stuffed Peppers

This vegetarian tapas dish is wonderfully tasty. Why not serve it alongside the Artichoke Hearts Marinated in Garlic (see page 103), Sautéed Lentils with Mushrooms (see page 117) and Patatas Bravas (see page 87) for a delicious vegetarian medley of tapas?

185 g/6 oz. canned piquillo peppers or pimientos

4 tbsp olive oil

3–4 garlic cloves, chopped

550 g/2 cups canned white beans, such as cannellini beans, part-drained, reserving the liquid

2 tbsp sherry vinegar (optional)

a handful of chopped fresh thyme or mint

salt and freshly ground black pepper

Serves 4

Drain the piquillo peppers and pat them dry with paper towels.

Heat the oil, garlic and part-drained white beans in a non-stick frying pan/skillet and mash with a fork to a thick, coarse purée. Add 1 tablespoon of the vinegar, if using, and 1 tablespoon of the reserved bean liquid, stir, then season well with salt and pepper. Let cool slightly, then stuff each piquillo with the mixture.

Sprinkle with the thyme, trickle over a tablespoon of the reserved bean liquid and a few drops of vinegar, if using, before serving.

Garlic Mushrooms

Sometimes the simplest of things can be the best. Plump, little button mushrooms fried in garlicky olive oil, and flavoured with lemon juice, salt and parsley, is a classic tapas dish in Spain for good reason. Serve with glasses of chilled fino or manzanilla sherry.

6 tbsp olive oil

2 garlic cloves, sliced across

200 g/7 oz. button mushrooms, ends of the stalks trimmed

freshly squeezed juice of ½ lemon

a small bunch of fresh flat-leaf parsley, finely chopped

salt

crusty bread, to serve

Serves 4

Heat the oil in a heavy-based frying pan/skillet.

Add the garlic and fry until golden, taking care not to let it burn. Add the mushrooms, lemon juice and salt, mixing well. Fry briefly over a high heat until the mushrooms are lightly browned.

Remove from the heat, stir in the parsley and serve at once with bread to mop up the garlicky juices.

Stuffed Mushrooms

These enticing stuffed mushrooms make an eye-catching addition to any tapas spread. Bear in mind that this recipe needs some forward planning as the stuffing needs to be left to marinate in the refrigerator overnight.

8 mushrooms

2 tbsp milk

2 tbsp fresh breadcrumbs

2 tbsp finely chopped onion

1 garlic clove, crushed

1 tbsp chopped fresh flat-leaf parsley

2 tbsp minced/ground pork

1 tbsp Serrano ham, finely chopped

1 tbsp canned chopped pimiento

1 tbsp freshly squeezed lemon juice

olive oil

Serves 4

Clean the mushrooms and remove the stalks. Finely chop 2 of the stalks and put them in a bowl. Add the milk and breadcrumbs and let soak for 10 minutes.

Add the onion, garlic, parsley, minced pork and Serrano ham. Mix well, cover with clingfilm/plastic wrap and let marinate in the refrigerator overnight.

Preheat the oven to 180°C (350°F) Gas 4.

Put the mushroom caps in an ovenproof dish and fill each with 1 heaped teaspoon of the mixture. Swirl over a little olive oil, then cook in the preheated oven for 15 minutes.

Remove from the oven, add a little chopped pimiento to each one and sprinkle with lemon juice.

Serve warm.

Sautéed Lentils with Mushrooms

Small brown lentils work well in this recipe because they stay firm during cooking, but the big green ones (castellanas) have a good flavour, too. Make this dish vegetarian by simply omitting the bacon.

250 g/1¼ cups small brown lentils,

rinsed 3 tbsp extra virgin olive oil

1 onion, finely chopped

1 garlic clove, crushed

25 g/2 tbsp butter

100 g/3½ oz. small chestnut/cremini mushrooms

100 g/3½ oz. oyster mushrooms, halved if large

3 tbsp chopped fresh flat-leaf parsley, plus extra to serve

1 tsp freshly squeezed lemon juice

6–12 slices of streaky bacon (optional)

salt and freshly ground black pepper

Serves 6

Put the lentils in a saucepan, cover with 1 litre/1 quart cold water and bring to the boil. Lower the heat and simmer for about 35 minutes or until tender (the time will depend on the age of the lentils). Drain well.

Heat 2 tablespoons of the oil in a frying pan/skillet, add the onion and garlic and sauté for 10 minutes until soft and pale golden. Add the butter, the remaining oil and the mushrooms. Stir-fry until the mushrooms are just cooked. Add the lentils, chopped parsley, lemon juice, and salt and pepper, and continue to stir over the heat until heated through.

Meanwhile, grill/broil the bacon until crisp.

Serve the lentils topped with some extra parsley and 1–2 slices of bacon per serving.

Spinach with Pine Nuts & Raisins

This tapas dish is frequently found in Catalonia and Andalusia. It is Moorish in origin. Feel free to add some onion or minced Serrano ham to the dish.

50 g/½ cup raisins

2 tbsp olive oil

25 g/½ cup pine nuts, toasted in a dry frying pan/skillet

2 garlic cloves, sliced

3 tbsp dry sherry

200 g/7 oz. spinach

a pinch of oak-smoked sweet Spanish paprika

salt and freshly ground black pepper

Serves 4

Soak the raisins in warm water for 3 minutes. Drain.

Heat the oil in a frying pan/skillet, add the pine nuts and garlic and cook for 1 minute. Add the sherry and boil for 1 minute.

Add the spinach and paprika and toss well to coat with the juices. Cook over a low heat for 5 minutes.

Add the drained raisins with salt and pepper to taste, then serve.

Spanish Tart with Peppers

This tart is called a coca and is like an open empanada, a bit like a pizza. It originates in Catalonia and the Balearics and is usually cooked in a communal outdoor stone or brick oven.

250 g/1⅔ cups plain/all-purpose flour

½ sachet easy-blend/fast-action dried yeast

½ tsp fine sea salt

TOPPING

4 tbsp extra virgin olive oil

2 large red onions, cut into wedges

about 500 g/1lb. 2 oz. canned piquillo peppers, drained

leaves from a small handful of fresh rosemary sprigs or fresh thyme

2 tbsp anchovy paste or purée, or canned anchovies, chopped and mashed

16 marinated anchovy fillets

a baking sheet, oiled

Serves 4–6

To make the dough, put the flour, yeast and salt in a bowl and mix. Add 150 ml/⅔ cup lukewarm water and mix to a satiny dough, then knead using a little extra flour, still in the bowl for 5 minutes or until silky. Cover the bowl with a cloth and leave in a warm place for about 1 hour, or until the dough has doubled in size.

Meanwhile, to make the topping, heat 3 tablespoons of the oil in a frying pan/skillet, add the onions and cook, stirring over a medium heat, until softened and transparent. Slice half the piquillos and add to the pan. Stir in most of the rosemary.

Preheat the oven to 220°C (425°F) Gas 7.

Transfer the dough to the oiled baking sheet. Punch down, flatten and roll out the dough to a 30-cm/12-inch circle. Snip, twist or roll the edges.

Spread the anchovy paste all over the top. Add the remaining whole piquillos and the cooked onion mixture. Arrange the anchovies and remaining rosemary on top and sprinkle with the remaining oil.

Bake in the preheated oven for 25–30 minutes until the base is crisp and risen, the edges golden and the filling hot and wilted. Serve in wedges, hot or cool.

Spanish Roasted Vegetables

2 red (bell) peppers

2 yellow or orange (bell) peppers

2 red onions, unpeeled

2 whole garlic heads

6–8 tbsp first cold-pressed extra virgin olive oil

4 slices of butternut squash or pumpkin, about 1.5 cm/ ½ inch thick, deseeded if necessary, or 2 large courgettes/zucchini, halved lengthways and scored with a fork

2 baby aubergines/eggplant or 1 large, sliced lengthways and scored with a fork

a small handful of fresh herbs, such as flat-leaf parsley, oregano, mint and thyme

salt and freshly ground black pepper

Serves 4

This dish, called *escalivada*, is deceptively simple. Its success depends on excellent olive oil and vegetables cooked in their skins for extra flavour.

Preheat the oven to 250°C (475°F) Gas 9.

Leave the stalks on the peppers, but remove and discard the seeds. Cut the unpeeled onions almost in half crossways, leaving one side joined, as a hinge.

Cut the unpeeled heads of garlic almost in half crossways, leaving a hinge of papery skin. Pour a teaspoon of the oil over the cut surfaces of the garlic, then put the bulbs back together again. Wrap up in foil, to make 2 packets.

Arrange all of the prepared vegetables, including the butternut squash and aubergines, in a single layer in 1–2 roasting pans, cut-sides uppermost. Sprinkle with 3–4 tablespoons of the oil.

Roast in the preheated oven for 35–40 minutes until soft and fragrant.

Transfer to a serving dish, sprinkle with the herbs, salt and pepper and the remaining oil. Serve hot or warm.

Vegetable Sauté

150 ml/⅔ cup extra virgin olive oil

2 onions, chopped

4 garlic cloves, finely chopped

½ tsp cumin seeds

2 aubergines/eggplant, chopped into 1-cm/½-inch cubes

6 tomatoes, skinned, deseeded and chopped, reserving any juices

300 g/10½ oz. courgettes/zucchini, cut into 1-cm/½-inch cubes

3 large roasted red (bell) peppers from a jar, cut into 1-cm/½-inch cubes

1 tbsp chopped fresh oregano, plus extra leaves to serve

2 tsp sherry vinegar or red wine vinegar

salt and freshly ground black pepper

Serves 4–6

This dish, known as *pisto Manchego*, from La Mancha in the heart of Spain, is probably based on an earlier Moorish aubergine/eggplant dish. The original didn't include tomatoes or peppers because these foods weren't introduced from the New World until the 16th century, after the expulsion of the Moors. This dish is very good eaten cold, but also works well warm. Serve it as part of a tapas spread with some fresh crusty bread alongside.

Heat half the oil in a heavy saucepan, add the onions and garlic and cook over a medium heat for 5 minutes until softened. Remove to a bowl.

Increase the heat and add the remaining oil. Add the cumin and aubergines, stir until they take up the oil and soften slightly, then add the tomatoes and their juices. Simmer until the mixture starts to thicken.

Fold in the courgettes, peppers and chopped oregano, season with salt and pepper and simmer gently, uncovered, until soft.

Fold in the vinegar and serve hot or cold with the oregano leaves sprinkled over.

INDEX

RECIPE CREDITS

VALERIE AIKMAN-SMITH
Padron Peppers

JULZ BERESFORD
Alioli
Artichoke Hearts Marinated in Garlic
Cheese Balls
Chicken with Garlic
Chorizo in Red Wine
Gazpacho
Lamb with Lemon
Marinated Anchovies
Marinated Octopus
Marinated Peppers
Marinated Sardines
Peppers Stuffed with Salt Cod
Pinchos
Prawns in Overcoats
Salt Cod Balls
Spicy Moorish Kebabs
Spinach with Pine Nuts & Raisins
Stuffed Mushrooms

ROSS DOBSON
Baked Mushrooms with Manchego
  Béchamel
Mussels with Fennel Aioli
Warm Marinated Olives

CLARE FERGUSON
Aubergine Cheese Fritters
Catalan Chickpeas & Chorizo
Spanish Clams with Serrano Ham
Spanish Potato Tortilla
Spanish Roasted Vegetables
Spanish Tart with Peppers
Squid with Aioli
Stuffed Peppers

JENNY LINFORD
Ajo Blanco
Chorizo Potato Salad
Garlic Mushrooms
Garlic Prawns
Ham & Mushroom Croquettes
Pan Catalan
Patatas Bravas
Potato Wedges with Romesco Sauce

LOUISE PICKFORD
Crispy Paella Balls with Romesco Sauce

ANNIE RIGG
Meatballs with Spiced Tomato Sauce

SHELAGH RYAN
Chorizo Tortilla Bites

JENNIE SHAPTER
Artichoke & Ham Tortilla
Mushroom & Pepper Tortilla

LINDY TUBBY
Artichokes with Serrano Ham
Baked Eggs Flamenco Style
Baked Sardines
Fried Cheese
Grilled Wild Asparagus
Hot Sandwiches
Migas with Serrano Ham
Potato Fritters with Chorizo
Sautéed Mushrooms with Lentils
Spinach & Salt Cod Tortilla
Stuffed Squid
Vegetable Sauté

PHOTOGRAPHY CREDITS

STEVE BAXTER
Pages 32 bottom right, 51.

MARTIN BRIGDALE
Pages 8 top right, 8 bottom left, 8 bottom right, 14, 19, 29, 30, 32 bl, 34, 38, 41, 42, 55, 58, 70, 73, 74, 90, 104, 107, 111, 116, 120, 123, 124.

PETER CASSIDY
Pages 5, 8 top left, 25, 26, 32 top left, 46, 49, 52, 56 top left, 56 tr, 61, 62, 65, 66, 69, 81, 84 bottom right, 84 top left, 94, 98, 102, 115, 119.

TARA FISHER
Pages 10, 17, 20.

JONATHON GREGSON
Pages 2, 108.

RICHARD JUNG
Page 23.

IAN WALLACE
Page 82.

KATE WHITAKER
Pages 13, 56 bottom right, 77, 101.

CLARE WINFIELD
Pages 6, 32 top right, 37, 45, 56 bottom left, 78, 84 top right, 86, 89, 93, 97, 112.